Haiti

by Joyce Markovics

Consultant: Karla Ruiz
Teachers College, Columbia University
New York, New York

BEARPORT PUBLISHING

New York, New York

Credits

Cover, © michaeljung/Shutterstock and © Kassia Marie Ott/Shutterstock; 3, © alexsvirid/Shutterstock; 4, © Necip Yanmaz/iStock; 5L, © glenda/Shutterstock; 5R, © arindambanerjee/Shutterstock; 7, © Necip Yanmaz/iStock; 8, © Keely Kernan/iStock; 9, ©Keely Kernan/iStock; 10, © Jay I. Kislak Collection Rare Book and Special Collections Division, Library of Congress; 11, © traveler1116/iStock; 12, © Everett Historical/Shutterstock; 13, © Everett Historical/Shutterstock; 14–15, © Louriv/Dreamstime; 16–17, © Necip Yanmaz/iStock; 17R, © Design Pics/Newscom; 18, © Michelle D. Milliman/Shutterstock; 18M, © jaminwell/iStock; 19, © Dawn J Benko/Shutterstock; 20, © glenda/Shutterstock; 21, © Michelle D. Milliman/Shutterstock; 22, © MaestroBooks/iStock; 23, © MaestroBooks/iStock; 24, © arindambanerjee/Shutterstock; 25, © Aaron Amat/Shutterstock; 26T, © Design Pics Inc/Alamy; 26B, © Singkham/Shutterstock; 27, © Lorg52/Dreamstime; 28, © All Canada Photos/Alamy; 29, © arindambanerjee/Shutterstock; 30T, © LMFotografia/Shutterstock; 30M, © Oleg_Mit/Shutterstock; 30B, © KSK Imaging/Shutterstock; 31 (T to B), © Louriv/Dreamstime, © Everett Historical/Shutterstock, and © glenda/Shutterstock.

Publisher: Kenn Goin
Senior Editor: Joyce Tavolacci
Creative Director: Spencer Brinker
Design: Debrah Kaiser
Photo Researcher: Olympia Shannon

Library of Congress Cataloging-in-Publication Data

Markovics, Joyce L., author.
  Haiti / by Joyce Markovics.
      pages cm. — (Countries we come from)
  Includes bibliographical references and index.
  Summary: "In this book, readers will be introduced to the country Haiti."—Provided by publisher.
  Audience: Ages 4–7.
  ISBN 978-1-943553-36-5 (library binding) — ISBN 1-943553-36-X (library binding)
  1. Haiti—Juvenile literature. I. Title.
  F1915.2.M37 2016
  972.94—dc23
                          2015029756

For more information, write to Bearport Publishing Company, Inc., 45 West 21st Street, Suite 3B, New York, New York 10010. Printed in the United States of America.

10 9 8 7 6 5 4 3 2 1

Contents

This Is Haiti

Colorful

WARM

Friendly

Haiti is a small **tropical** country. It's located on an island called Hispaniola.

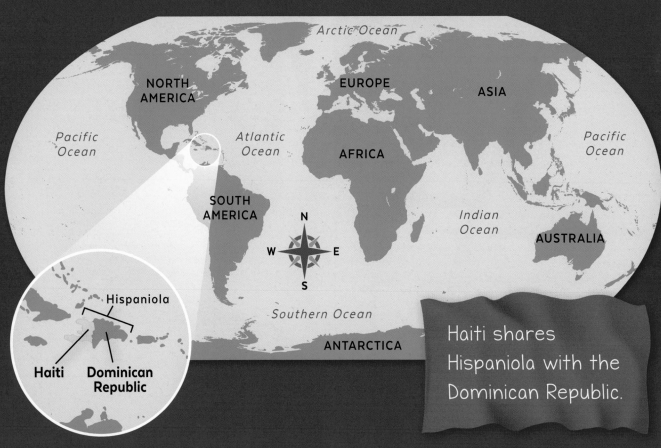

Arctic Ocean

NORTH AMERICA

EUROPE

ASIA

Pacific Ocean

Atlantic Ocean

AFRICA

Pacific Ocean

SOUTH AMERICA

Indian Ocean

AUSTRALIA

N
W   E
S

Southern Ocean

ANTARCTICA

Hispaniola

Haiti   Dominican Republic

Haiti shares Hispaniola with the Dominican Republic.

More than ten million people live in Haiti.

Haiti is warm and breezy for most of the year.

There are miles of sandy beaches.

There are also tall mountains.
They stretch across the land.

The name *Haiti* means "land of the mountains."

The first people to live in Haiti were called the Taíno (TYE-noh).

a rock figure carved by the Taíno people

a Taíno stool

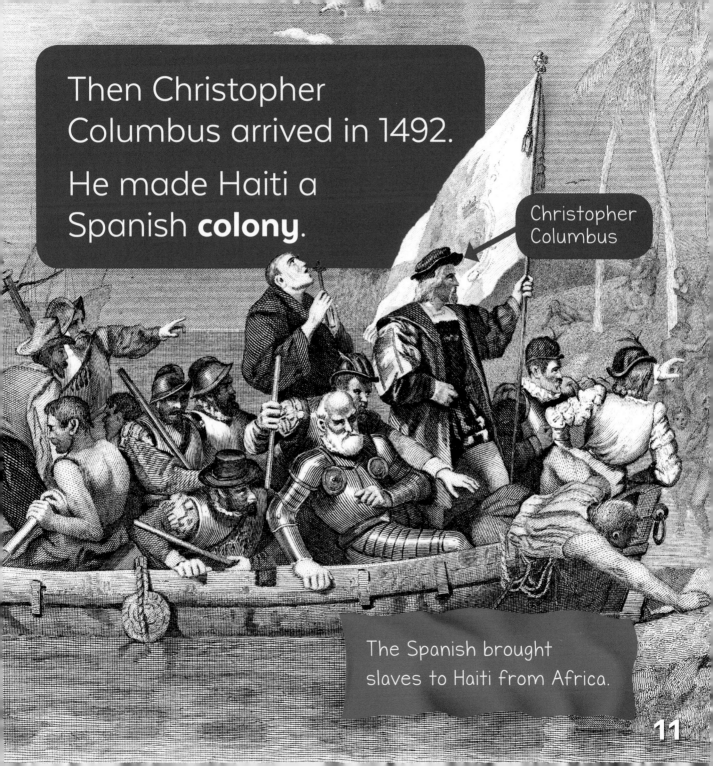

Then Christopher Columbus arrived in 1492.

He made Haiti a Spanish **colony**.

Christopher Columbus

The Spanish brought slaves to Haiti from Africa.

11

In the 1600s, Haiti became a French colony.

The slaves rose up against the French.

After a long war, the slaves won.

Haiti became its own country in 1804.

A man named Toussaint L'Ouverture (too-SAN loo-ver-TUR) helped Haiti gain its freedom.

Toussaint L'Ouverture

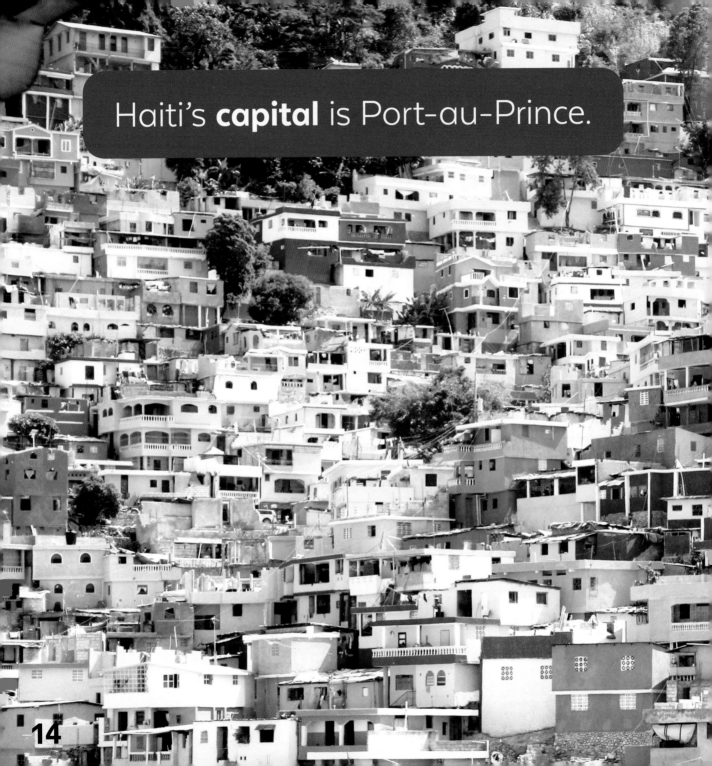

Haiti's **capital** is Port-au-Prince.

It's the biggest city in the country.

Half of all Haitians live in Port-au-Prince.

15

A huge **earthquake** struck Haiti in 2010.

Thousands of people were killed.

Many more lost their homes.

Haitians are working to rebuild their country.

Many Haitians work as farmers. They grow mangoes, bananas, and other fruit.

mangoes

Most of Haiti's land is used for farming.

18

Farmers also raise animals such as pigs.

Most Haitians speak Creole, and some speak French.

This is how you say *hello* in Creole:

Bonjou (bawn-ZHOO)

This is how you say *hello* in French:
Bonjour (bawn-ZHOOR)

Creole is similar to French.

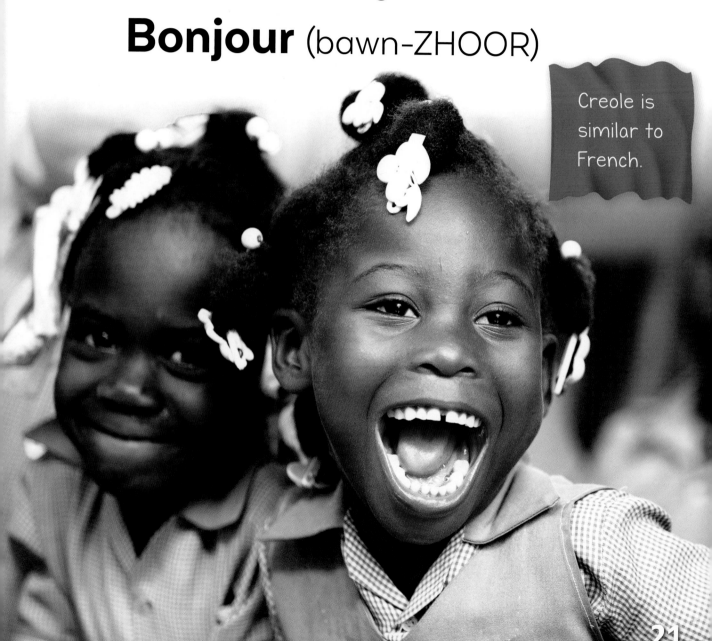

Haiti has many celebrations.

Carnival is one of the most popular.

Kanaval is the Creole word for "carnival."

People make large, colorful masks.
They dance and sing in the streets.

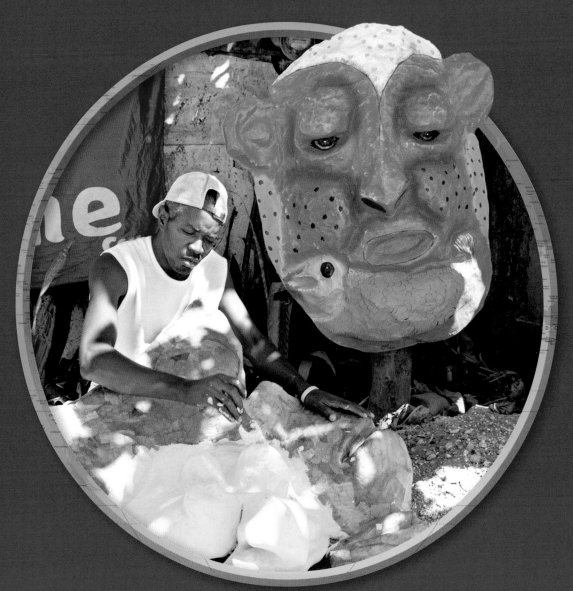

Haitians love sports—especially soccer. Teams play around the country.

Basketball is also a popular sport.

What do people like to eat in Haiti?

Rice and beans is a popular dish.

Many Haitians eat manioc (MAN–ee–ahk). It's a tree root that has been cooked.

People also make and enjoy spicy stews.

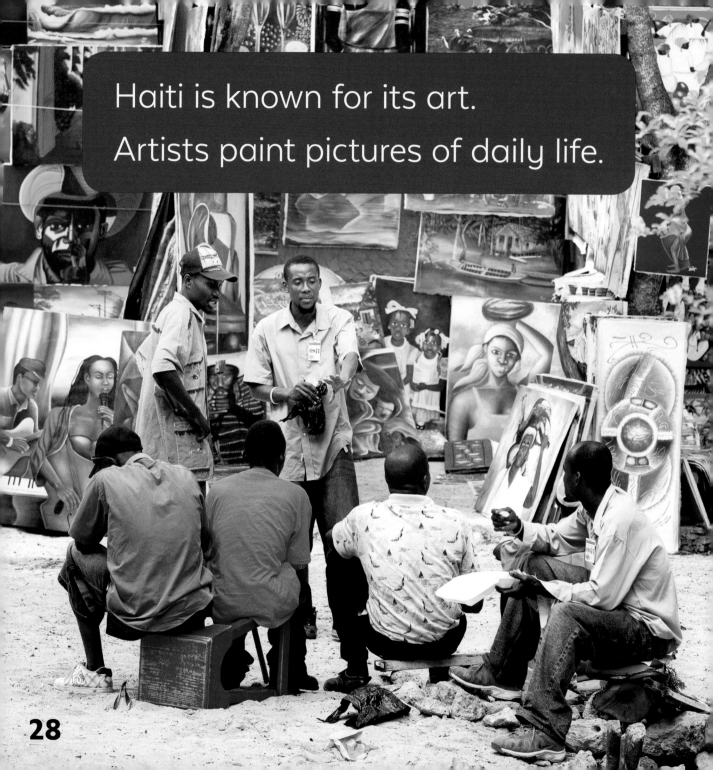

Haiti is known for its art.

Artists paint pictures of daily life.

They use old pieces of metal to make beautiful objects!

Haitians often use bright colors in their art.

Fast Facts

Capital city:
Port-au-Prince

Population of Haiti:
More than ten million

Main languages:
French and Creole

Money: Gourde

Major religions: Roman Catholic,
Protestant, Voodoo, and other religions

Neighboring country:
The Dominican Republic

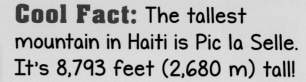

Cool Fact: The tallest
mountain in Haiti is Pic la Selle.
It's 8,793 feet (2,680 m) tall!

capital (KAP-uh-tuhl) a city where a country's government is based

colony (KOL-uh-nee) an area that has been settled by people from another country and is ruled by that country

earthquake (URTH-*kwayk*) a sudden shaking of the ground caused by the movement of Earth's outer layer

tropical (TROP-i-kuhl) having to do with the warm areas of Earth near the equator

Index

Read More

Bartell, Jim. *Haiti (Blastoff! Readers: Exploring Countries).* Minneapolis, MN: Bellwether Media (2011).

Raum, Elizabeth. *Haiti (Countries Around the World).* Chicago: Heinemann (2012).

Learn More Online

To learn more about Haiti, visit
www.bearportpublishing.com/CountriesWeComeFrom

About the Author

Joyce Markovics has written many books for young readers. She lives along the beautiful Hudson River in Ossining, New York.